MECHANICS-
MERCANTILE
LIBRARY.

Arthur F. Mathews '06

All Afloat on Noah's Boat!

To Scarlet Pleasence
& to all who would be butterflies under the rainbow – T.M.

To the superstars Frank, Billy, and Lucas – G.P-R.

Text copyright © 2006 by Tony Mitton
Illustrations copyright © 2006 by Guy Parker-Rees
First published in Great Britian in 2006 by Orchard Books London.
Library of Congress Cataloging-in-Publication Data
Mitton, Tony All Afloat on Noah's Boat! / by Tony Mitton; art by Guy Parker-Rees.
–1st ed. p. cm. Summary: When the animals on board Noah's ark begin to get bored
and restless, he stages a talent show featuring the various creatures.
[1. Animals–Fiction. 2. Noah's ark–Fiction. 3. Talent shows–Fiction. 4. Stories in rhyme.]
I. Parker-Rees, Guy, ill. II. Title. PZ8.3.M685Al 2007 [E]–dc22 2006023635
ISBN 13: 978-0-439-87397-0 / ISBN 10: 0-439-87397-5 (alk. paper)
10 9 8 7 6 5 4 3 2 1   08 09 10 11
Printed in China / Reinforced Binding for Library Use / First U.S. Edition, May 2007

All Afloat on Noah's Boat!

TONY MITTON ★ GUY PARKER-REES

Orchard Books · New York
an imprint of Scholastic Inc.

Bang bang,

tap tap,

chip chip chip!

Noah built a house in the shape of a ship.

He built it wide and he built it tall.

He built it for creatures great and small.

When the rain came down, Noah clanged his bell
crying, "All aboard the Ark Hotel!
The ground's getting wet. It'll soon be mud.
Come and keep safe
from the rising flood."

So, along came the creatures, all in pairs,
flying through the windows, stepping up the stairs,
filling up the Ark with a racket and a row.
There were snakes in the stern
and bears in the bow.

The rain rattled down on the great big boat,

till the water rose and made it float.

All they could see was flood and sky,
but aboard Noah's Ark they were safe and dry.

Well, the days went by
and the weeks went past,

and it seemed that the
flood would last and last.

All those creatures,
packed so tight,
got bored and snappy
till they felt like a fight.

The lions and the leopards turned mean and catty.

And, boy, those rodents sure were ratty!

There were animal **tantrums**

and insect miffs

and the birds started
trilling out twittery tiffs.

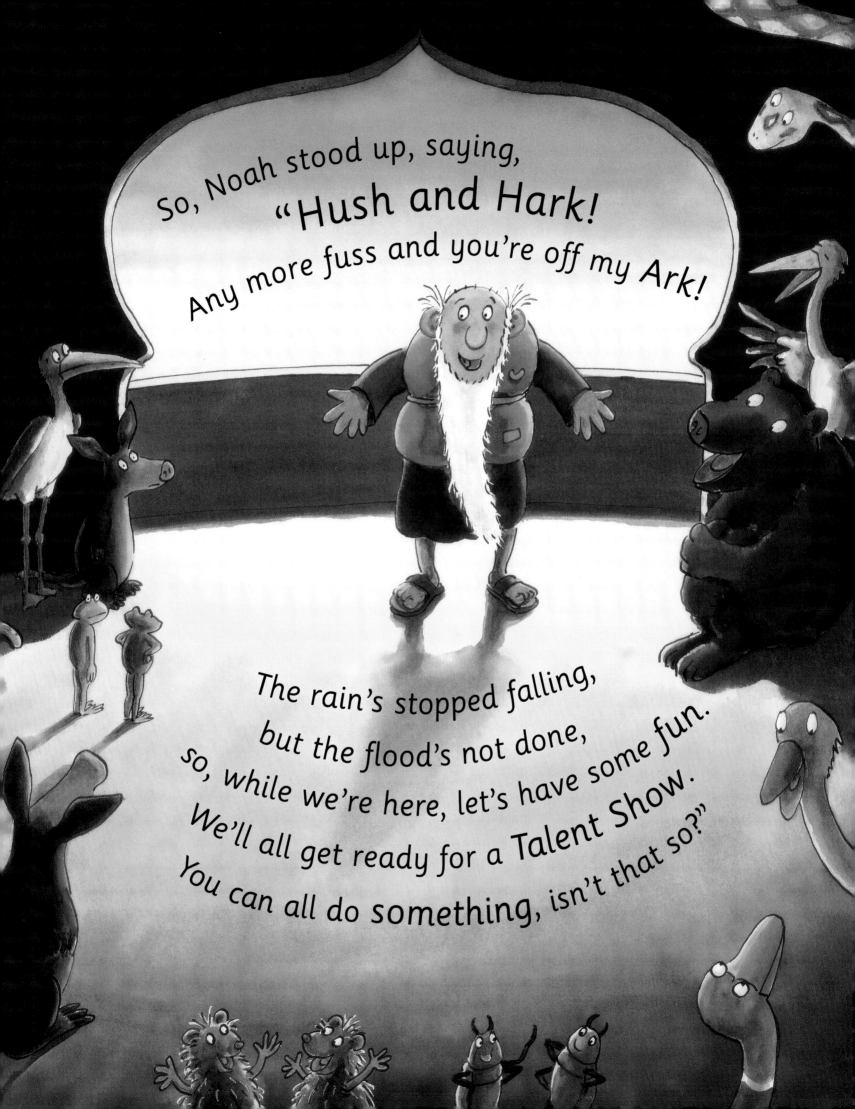

Clever old Noah.
That did the trick.
There were no more quarrels
or fights to pick.

When at last it was time
to begin the show,
old Noah said, "Well?
Are you ready?

So, the animals came on
two by two,
to show the things
that they could do.

Go!"

The frogs sprang on doing hyper-hops.

They flipped all **over** the tabletops.

The toucans played a rhythmic peck, with tapping beaks, upon the deck.

The elephants dipped their trunks in the sea

And blew high fountains — ready?

Wheeeeeeeeeee.

But nobody heard
the caterpillars croon,

"We're wrapping ourselves
in a tight cocoon."

The snakes
both tied
themselves
in knots.

The leopards
wiggled
all their spots.

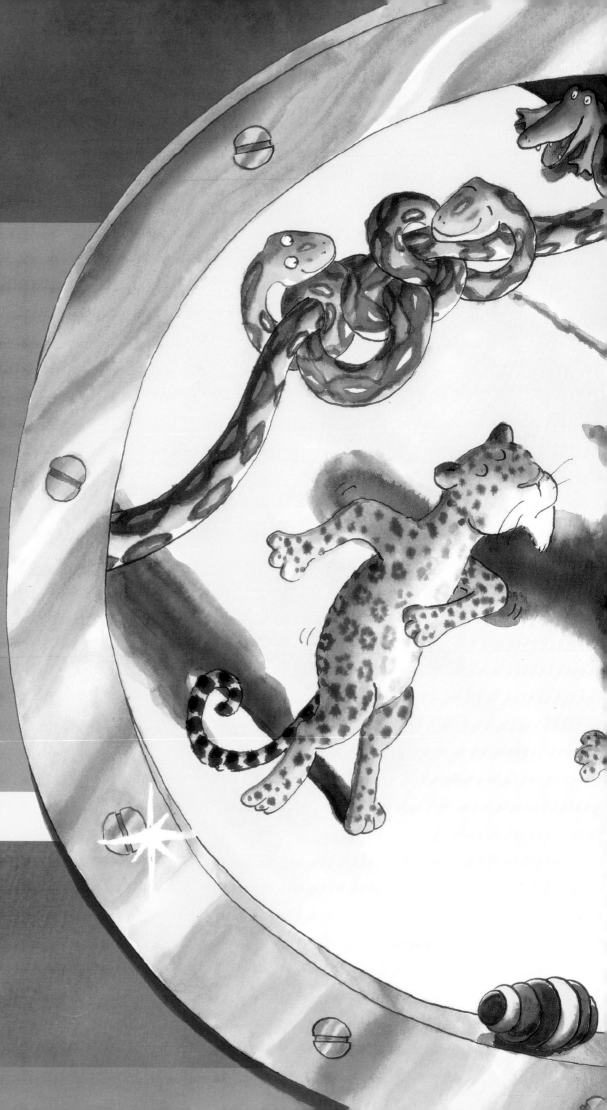

Oh, what a
rumpus!
Oh, what a
row!

That Talent Show
got busy now!

But the poor
little caterpillars
lay quite still,
all wrapped up on
the windowsill.

The
crocodiles
balanced
on the
tips of
their
tails.

The monkeys screeched out

mega-wails.

The Talent Show
was such a ball,
There's not the space
to tell it all.

And the caterpillars thought,
"They're all so good.
We'd both join in
if we only could."

But when the show was nearly through,
Noah whispered, "One more act to do . . . "

Each caterpillar's tight cocoon
looked like it might crack open soon . . .

Then out they burst! Surprise! Surprise!

They'd both turned into **butterflies!**

They spread their brilliant wings out wide
and every single creature sighed.

"They're **beautiful**!" said Noah. "Oh, my!
They've opened up their wings to fly.
But look — out there the water's **gone**!
That means there's **land** to live upon."

"The butterflies can end our show.
Let's wave good-bye and watch them go . . . "

Then the creatures came out, two by two,
on a world that waited, bright and new.